THE TOP 12 MISTAKES PEOPLE MAKE WITH THEIR IMMIGRATION CASES

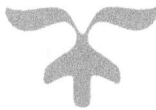

AND HOW TO AVOID THEM

ABRAHAM B. CARDENAS, ESQUIRE

Table of Contents

Introduction

Every immigration case—even the simplest of cases—is a journey through a vast maze of complex immigrations laws, which is full of twists and turns. With an immigration case, the road to success is full of obstacles, road blocks, detours, and dead ends. You need to know how to navigate through this system, so you can avoid the mistakes that can get you lost within it. To have the best possibility of reaching success in your case, you need information.

After 25 years of experience as an immigration attorney, I have that information, and I feel I must share it. This information is unique, and it's intended to guide you through your immigration journey—with the goal of obtaining a successful outcome. This information could benefit thousands of lives, including you and/or your family.

Where are you with your immigration case right now? Are your discouraged? Maybe you feel you don't know how to proceed. How long will it take? How much does it all cost? Do you worry that what you are doing is not going to be enough? And is it correct? Have you hit a wall with letters that you've received from the immigration authorities?

Whether you are just starting a case, are now in middle of a case, or are planning on starting a case in the future, this book will greatly benefit you with rich information, which will show you the most common mistakes people make and how you can avoid them. You will learn from the errors others have made. My experience will enlighten you about the right path to follow in moving your case through the U.S. immigration system.

This book has evolved out of the frustration I've experienced as an immigration attorney—seeing all of the mistakes people make when dealing with their immigration cases. I've consulted with thousands of clients and have seen every type of error. It's crazy how easily some of these mistakes could have been avoided. Some mistakes were made by underestimating the complexity of the immigration laws, and others were due to ignorance of the system. Still other mistakes were based on incorrect assumptions, and yet others were made because people thought they could get away with deception. This book is intended to give you knowledge and information about how to easily avoid these common mistakes which are seen every day in the immigration system.

Each chapter gives examples of the most common errors. In a no-nonsense, easy-to-understand way, I then explain things that you must know about the immigration laws—and that will illuminate your way through your case. This book is not meant to be a law book with cases and citations. Instead, it is a down-to-earth explanation of legal concepts, procedures, and instructions. You will find answers to many questions. You will discover information you need, in order to improve your chance of success. I'll also warn you how to avoid anything that could be construed as fraud or the concealment of information.

By the time you reach the end of this book, you will have knowledge, encouragement, and a better understanding of what to do, how to do it right, and what to avoid. With an open mind, attention, and patience, you will begin your path to a better possibility of winning your case. You will avoid errors, and your process will flourish as information lights your way. You will begin to overcome any fears you may have, and you'll take the actions needed to achieve your goal. So turn the page and begin now!

Chapter 1:
Typical Application Errors

"Your best teacher is your last mistake."

Ralph Nader

The most common interaction a person will have with the immigration authorities is when filing one of the many applications that they process. Probably the #1 reason for problems when filing applications or petitions with the immigration authorities is due to some kind of error in the paperwork.

These applications can sometimes be complex, and anyone can make an error when filling them out. The truth is that even lawyers sometimes make errors when filling them out. The difference is that the chances that a lawyer will make a mistake are significantly diminished due to experience. We learn from our mistakes, and we almost always only make a mistake once. Experienced lawyers rarely ever make a mistake.

Imagine a person doing an application for the first—and probably only—time in their life. They usually don't know how to do it, and they are learning as they go. An experienced immigration lawyer files applications every week, and sometimes files similar applications every day. When a lawyer makes a mistake in an application, most of the time the error is something minimal, and it can be corrected without much of a problem. When a person who has filled out their own application makes a mistake, the most likely way that they are going to know that the

1

mistake has happened is when they receive a denial letter about that application.

When I'm asked whether someone needs a lawyer or not that, the mistake ratio is one of the reasons that I now advise almost all my potential clients that they should get a lawyer. The level of complexity in some of these applications is very high. The need for a lawyer is evident. And it's not getting any easier. For example, the form to apply for naturalization (N-400) was just recently updated, and it went from 10 pages to 21 pages! Other forms are getting updated soon, and they are not getting shorter or easier.

Common Mistakes When Filing

If you are going to file an application on your own, then you must know the most common mistakes people make when they file something with the United States Citizenship and Immigration Service (USCIS) or any other immigration-related agency:

1. Not double-checking your application.

In my office, for every application that I prepare and/or sent out, I check the application, and my paralegal checks the application. And I give it to my client to sit down and check, so that we can make any corrections needed right there and then—before anything gets sent to Immigration. The reason that I follow this process is to minimize and eliminate all errors. Always double and triple-check your applications.

I have some clients that do their own forms, but they hire me to check them over before they send them. I can't tell you that all kinds of problems have been avoided just by them doing this.

2. Not sending the correct forms.

I can't tell you how many times I've had clients come into the office after they've done their own paperwork. Or they've had some local "notario" or paralegal office do the paperwork for them. And we discover that the wrong application form was sent in. Of course, this is an indication that whoever filled it out didn't know what they were doing.

Understanding the immigration process requires knowing exactly what forms to use, which vary depending on what you're applying for. Avoiding this grave mistake can eliminate stress and aggravation when dealing with a person's case.

Get help if you need it, but make sure to find out exactly which form to use. Regardless, USCIS will charge the fee you send them, and they'll eventually deny the application. There is no refund. Even worse, sometimes the denial takes months or even years to process after the original application, and all that time is lost.

3. Not sending the correct supporting documents.

Filling out an application is one thing; I always say that any 14-year-old can fill out most applications without much trouble. But making sure that the application is sent with all the supporting documents is another thing. One has to know exactly what has to be sent with the application.

If the wrong documents are sent—or documents are missing from the application—then the consequence could be a lengthy delay in the process, or even a denial of the case. Some applications require a great deal of paperwork, and some don't. You need to know the difference.

4. Not sending the correct fee.

Many times, people fill out the forms, but they forget to add the fee to the application when they send it. Other times, they send a fee, but it is the incorrect fee. Knowing what fee to send—and whether a fee has to be sent at all—is important. Once again, not sending a fee will cause the application to be delayed or sent back, and important deadlines may be missed as a result. Another very important point is that if you pay your fee with a personal check, make sure that the check is valid, and there are enough funds in the bank.

I recently had a case, in which I prepared an application for the legal permanent resident status of a client. My practice is to give the application package to the client to mail. She included a check to pay the fee for the application. Her problems started because the check bounced when USCIS attempted to cash it. And of course, the application was put on hold. USCIS gave her an opportunity to write another check, but she only had a certain amount of time to send the new funds. She waited until the last minute to resend the correct fee with a money order.

Nevertheless, everything seemed to be going well. While we waited for her case to be processed, we were able to apply for her employment authorization document.

When we went to apply for the document a second time a year later, it was denied because USCIS thought that the filing fee for the original application was never paid. Had she written a valid check at the very beginning, she would have avoided all of the aggravation that came after that. We had to expend a great deal of time (and she had to spend a great deal of additional expense) proving to the USCIS that the fee had been paid. Even though they got the funds and cashed the money order, we had to do all of the running around to prove that they had gotten the money.

5.   Not filing a change of address.

I cannot stress enough how important it is for the immigration authorities to have a current, valid address for every person that has filed any kind of document with them. Over the years, I have seen many applications denied or considered abandoned because the client never notified the immigration authorities of a change of address. As a result, they never received notifications that were sent out; either Immigration was asking for additional information or notifying them of an additional step that needed to be taken.

It is important to always notify Immigration of a new address when you move, whether you are the applicant or the beneficiary. In our office, we do changes of address as part of the services we offer for any application we do. If you don't know how to do it, find help, but do it immediately.

6. Not making copies of everything sent to the Immigration authorities.

One of the most frustrating things that I encounter when I am consulting with a potential client—

or when I've taken on a new case where applications have previously been filed by the client or certain notario offices—is discovering that no copies of those filed applications have been made. Knowing what information has been sent to the immigration authorities in the application or petition is very important. Not having copies of everything that was sent can cause delays or be very problematic for anything that is being done in the future, regarding a person's case.

The standard practice in my office is to make a copy of every single document in an application that is being sent to the immigration authorities. I even make copies of the envelopes that the paperwork is being mailed in. I give a copy of all that to my client, so that they have it for their records. And of course, I keep electronic copies of everything for myself, so that I can access it from anywhere.

7.   Using incorrect or out-of-date forms.

The immigration authorities are now constantly updating or changing the forms that they require that applicants or petitioners use when they send them in. One common error I see is people using outdated forms for their applications or petitions with USCIS. These forms are updated and available at the website for the immigration authorities. Most forms can be found at www.uscis.gov. Any use of outdated forms is usually considered inexcusable.

8.   Filing the wrong address.

Even now after 25 years of practicing law, I make it a habit to always double-check the USCIS website for the address that an application or petition has been sent to. The reason is because these addresses have been known to change from time to time. Again, this information is available on the website, so the immigration authority will receive the paperwork.

9.   Missing a deadline in error.

In certain applications or petitions, there are tight deadlines that have to be met, in order to qualify for a benefit. Any of the mistakes listed above can result in missing a deadline, and perhaps in losing the one and only opportunity for the filing. This is very true with appeals and motions to reopen or reconsider. If you miss the deadline, even if by error, you almost certainly won't be given a second chance. This a lawyer's worse nightmare.

The immigration system is very unforgiving with deadlines. They have to be. Think about it for a minute: They deal with tens of thousands of cases during any given week, and they don't have the time or resources to deal with every single mistake someone has made. They can't be "nice" to you, because then they have to do the same with everyone else. Having strict guidelines helps keep an already overburdened system working as smoothly as possible. Make sure you know your deadline.

Do not make the mistake of thinking that mailing something by the deadline means you have met the deadline. Make sure the proper agency gets the application before the date specified for the deadline. Send it by express courier if necessary. And remember that even if the mistake of missing a deadline is not your fault, the application will still be considered late and rejected. Don't wait until the last minute to file.

Chapter 2:
Not Preparing for Your Case

"By failing to prepare, you are preparing to fail."

Benjamin Franklin

Most likely, almost every person in the United States who is not a US citizen has a case, either pending or likely to be starting in the future. Even a legal permanent resident will hopefully file for his or her citizenship one day. Preparation for that case is very important. In the practice of immigration law, one big error that I have seen over the years is when individuals come to see me, but they are completely unprepared for their case. They've never given it any thought. They're seeing me because they are now dealing with a case (like a deportation proceeding), or because they finally want to start a case and need help with it.

Preparing for a Future Case

If you are in the United States and you know that you're going to have a case with Immigration sometime in the future, the best thing that you can do is begin preparing for that case now. Preparation can make any future filing (or emergency) so much easier to deal with. Some examples of these kinds of cases may be a future application for citizenship, a future application for legal permanent resident status, a future deportation proceeding, or a future petition for a family relative. These are only a few examples, and there are so many more possibilities.

The very first thing you should do to begin preparing for a future case now is to seek out professional, legal advice with an experienced immigration attorney. You want to do this, so you will be educated about what is involved. That way, you know what is necessary down the line for the case.

You should begin by saving evidence of everything. Don't throw out important (or even not-so-important) papers. Get a box, and start putting things in there: medical records, school records, important purchases (such as a car), real estate documents, leases, cancelled checks, bank statements, and credit card statements. The list goes on and on. Save any paperwork that shows community activities, or any other type of evidence that proves that you are intimately involved in your community. Do you donate to your church or other organization? Save the proof. Do you send money to your family back home? Keep the receipts of money transfers. You want to show all of your activities in the U.S., which will demonstrate what you have been doing here, and for how long.

In addition to the type of paperwork listed above, you want to also keep all of your important documents in a safe location. These include things like birth certificates, marriage certificates, divorce decrees (all of them), death certificates, deeds, car titles, adoption records, passports, and other such important "life event" documents. I would also suggest that you have good color copies made of them, and keep them somewhere else—with a trusted family member or friend. I would even go so far as to suggest that you scan these documents and save them to a file storage account on the internet (with applications from Google, Dropbox, or Microsoft OneDrive). Having copies of these important documents can make it so much easier to get new ones, if for some reason they are lost or destroyed.

One very important piece of evidence that is vital to many types of immigration cases is having proof of filing income tax returns. In immigration cases, I have seen judges strongly scold respondents in an open-courtroom hearing because they did not file their income taxes. I have also seen judges use the fact that the respondent filed taxes consistently every year as a favorable factor in their discretion to grant a relief, which was being sought before the court.

For a naturalization application to be granted so you can get your citizenship, you must state on that application— and be prepared to prove—that all of your tax returns have been filed as required. Everybody needs to file taxes. It doesn't matter if you are here in the country legally or without papers. If you are not here legally, you still have to file tax returns. Get yourself an Individual Tax Identification Number (ITIN) from the IRS, and file them. I have included a separate chapter on this topic alone, because it is so important.

Preparing for a Present or Current Case

When preparing for a case that you currently have in front of an Immigration Court, USCIS, or any other immigration agency, you need to know how to prepare for that case. Again, the best way to learn about your specific situation is by talking to an attorney: This person can counsel you about what documentation you need, and how to go about preparing and defending your case.

In most cases, the first thing that you start with is official documents, such as certified copies of birth certificates, marriage certificates, divorce decrees, death certificates, criminal records, and tax returns. If your case involves proving a hardship to a family member (such as a waiver application), you need to get evidence of that hardship. Evidence of a hardship may include medical records, income records, and statements from friends and family.

If you're doing these cases with the assistance of an attorney, you are actually an assistant to your attorney when preparing. A good immigration attorney will instruct you about what type of documentation you need. When I take on an immigration case, one of the very first things I do with my clients is advise them about what documentation I need in the preparation of their cases. I also educate them in detail about exactly what we are going to be doing together—to help them avoid deportation or apply for any kind of benefit. Educating my clients is vital, so they understand what it is that we are doing and what we need to do it.

Preparing for the Costs

One area of frustration that many clients encounter when they come to me for help is not having the funds necessary to do the work that needs to be done to help them throughout their case. Whenever I counsel any client that has a case in the future, I make them aware of the filing cost for the relief they are seeking, as well as what the cost for an attorney is going to be. This way, they are prepared for those costs whenever they start their cases, or whenever the costs need to be presented.

One of the worst things that could happen when someone confronts their immigration case, especially if it's sudden, is not having the money to properly pursue an application or defend against deportation. I have seen people with very good cases give up and allow a deportation, because they just didn't have the money to hire a good lawyer to help them. It is a lot easier to prepare for something when you have plenty of time than it is to suddenly be caught in a situation and have to scramble to get documents and money, in order to do something correctly. Start saving money now. Be ready.

I had a client that came to consult with me regarding her case. She knew that she was going to eventually be facing a deportation case. She wanted to know what she could do now, in case she was detained. I gave her all of the details. The years went by, and little by little, she saved for the inevitable.

One day while she was at work, the immigration authorities raided the factory, and she was detained. Because she was financially prepared, she was able to immediately hire me to take over her case. She was able to pay for her bond, which I obtained for her within days. And we started her deportation defense. She was also prepared with paperwork. Most of the others that were detained at her job were deported.

It took over three years, but I was able to win her case. And she was able to get her green card. Today, she is a U.S. citizen. She was able to petition for her mother and other family members to reunite in the U.S. Everyone should follow her example and be prepared.

Summary

Once again, preparation is very important to most immigration cases, and financial preparation is just as important as gathering documents. Avoiding problems with a case involves preparing for that case. Save yourself the stress, aggravation, and heartache by starting now.

Chapter 3:
Missing a Hearing or Interview

"The world is run by those who show up."

– Author Unknown

Missing Court Hearings or Interviews with USCIS

I'm sure that anyone reading this can imagine that missing a court hearing, an interview for an immigration petition, or an application is almost always fatal. Usually, the result is a deportation order from an Immigration Court, or the denial of an application or petition with USCIS or other immigration authority.

Some common mistakes that cause certain people to miss their hearings or interviews include something simple, like not having provided a correct address to the immigration agency handling your case—and not getting hearing or meeting notifications because of that. Keeping the immigration authorities up-to-date with your current address is not only the law, it also benefits you.

I always recommend that when my clients move or change their address, they come to me immediately. That way, we can fill out the proper paperwork to notify the proper agency, court, or other immigration authority. After that, I

15

encourage them to make sure that they are properly registered with the post office at their current address. Several times, I've had clients tell me that they are concerned about the safety of their mail arriving at their address. If that is the case, I encourage them to get a post office box or a secure address, where they can get mail sent from the immigration authorities.

The government must always have the address where you live. You can always provide them with a mailing address, in addition to the address of your residence. I also suggest that my clients go to their local post office to make sure that their name is properly registered as the address they are using. This is because certain mail, including any mail from USCIS or other immigration agencies, is not supposed to be placed in a mailbox—when the addressee is not listed as living at that location. The post office is instructed to return mail from the government, rather than forward it to a new address, because certain government mail is not supposed to be forwarded.

Don't Ever Miss a Court Hearing

Missing a hearing with the Immigration Court will most likely result in an order of deportation issued by the Immigration Judge. This is called an in-absentia order. If a person gets an in-absentia order, it is difficult to undo the damage. But even so, there may be a way to reverse it. This is done by way of a motion to reopen.

If you missed a court hearing, go see an immigration attorney immediately. This is something that you should never try to do without an immigration attorney, who knows how to prepare this type of motion before the court. It is important to remember that if this happens to someone, they should act quickly because there is only a set amount of time that a person has to file a motion to reopen. The sooner a motion to reopen is completed with the court, the more likely it is that the motion will be granted. However, this is contingent on you having a very good, reasonable explanation for why you missed the hearing in the first place. Still, the best way to avoid any problems with an Immigration Court is to never miss a hearing.

Missing a Hearing with USCIS or Other Agency

If a hearing is missed with the United States Citizenship and Immigration Service Office, the usual result is that any application or petition is denied. Normally, there is no way to reopen that case. There may be a possibility to file a Motion to Reconsider, but that is a costly move. And in most cases, it's not worth the expense. But a good immigration attorney can help you determine if you can do this in your case.

In most instances, the person has to refile the application. In some cases, they may not even be able to refile. This is because there are certain applications that have specific deadlines associated with them. If the application is filed on time—but is denied later because of a missed interview or hearing—it is almost always likely that you cannot refile because the deadline was missed. This is why it is important to work with an attorney when you have a case with Immigration.

In all of my cases, I always instruct my clients about the importance of showing up to their appointments or hearings. I also advise them about the severe consequences of missing an appointment or hearing. If whatever application or legal process we are doing in court or with an agency is a one-time-only opportunity, I make it very clear to my client that the consequences of missing any hearing, appointment, or interview would be fatal to their case.

The #1 reason for people missing their appointments or hearings is simple fear. I have a chapter in this book devoted to the subject of fear. However, most of the time, the fear is unfounded. Having an attorney by your side for your case can help to get rid of fear. One of the ways that I help my clients deal with their fears is educating them. I give them information. I let them know what all the possibilities are. I have found that the more information that my client has and the more I educate them about their case, the less fear they have. I also encourage them to let me know what they think might be causing their fear. This way, I can address those fears or concerns, and help them to get rid of them or reduce them.

Summary

The consequences of missing a hearing, appointment, or interview are severe and devastating to a case. Making sure you never miss an appointment is crucial. To make sure you get your notices, always update your address with immigration authorities. If you ever do miss an appointment, immediately go and consult with an immigration attorney to determine if there is a way to remedy the consequences.

Chapter 4:
Lying About or Hiding
Information

*He who permits himself to tell a lie once, finds it much
easier to do it a second and third time, till at length it
becomes habitual; he tells lies without attending to it,
and truths without the world's believing him. This
falsehood of the tongue leads to that of the heart, and in
time depraves all its good dispositions.*

- **THOMAS JEFFERSON**

Immigration Officers and judges are professionally trained
to detect fraud. Because fraud is such a big problem with
many immigration processes that they encounter, a good
part of their training involves detecting lying and
deception. They know how to sniff out when a person is
lying, or when he or she is hiding information.

We all have a common-sense understanding of what fraud
is. Usually when we think of fraud, we imagine someone
who is lying, someone who is deliberately concealing
information, or someone who is just overtly doing
something evil or wrong to defraud someone else. The
immigration laws also see it that way. However, the way
the immigration laws are applied may also include
seemingly innocent acts that are interpreted as fraud, even
though they are not fraud in the traditional sense.

A simple example would be an unmarried daughter who
received a travel visa to come into the United States

because her mother petitioned for her. She goes to the embassy and picks up her visa. In an effort to show her true love to her long-time boyfriend, she marries him two days before she gets on the airplane to go to the United States. She enters on a visa that was meant for an unmarried child of a U.S. citizen, but she is now married. Years later, she either goes to apply for her citizenship, or she petitions for her husband. And it is discovered that she was married when she entered the U.S. on a visa that was meant for an unmarried child of a U.S. citizen. The immigration authorities see this as fraud. She clearly did not intend to defraud the government. However, by marrying before she entered the U.S., that was what she did—as interpreted by the immigration laws.

My years of experience have led me to the conclusion that lying to immigration authorities—or concealing information from them—is probably one of the most dangerous, foolish mistakes my clients make. This is even truer now, since technology has become so advanced. The level of sophistication of computer programs and hardware the government is using for investigation is getting higher and higher every day. They are able to reach into the databases of other agencies and organizations that hold information, which may contradict or expose the hiding or lying that is being done by the client. Even now, when I go to the interviews or hearings with my clients, my jaw drops when I see the type of information that the government reveals. I sit there and scratch my head, saying, "How did they find that out?"

But exposing fraud doesn't always require sophisticated technology. In a case I had recently, my client petitioned for his wife, who was outside of the United States. These processes can sometimes take anywhere from a year to two years, depending on the country. At one point, he was scheduled for an interview at the local USCIS office. When he showed up to the interview, he was confronted with photos from his Facebook account, showing him with another woman. He was questioned about her. He tried to explain himself, saying that he was in a relationship with her prior to his current marriage. But as you can imagine, it did not go very well for him in that interview. He was left hanging—with uncertainty about whether or not his application was going to be approved or denied. Only then did he go see a lawyer.

I had another client who was being petitioned by her husband, and they both lived here in the United States. At the interview, she was confronted with the fact that the official that married them was using her address for some obscure licensing application, which he'd done a long time prior to that. We spent a great deal of time gathering evidence and filling out paperwork. We were trying to convince the immigration officer that this man was a long-time family friend, that she allowed him to use the home address for this licensing, and that he was not in any kind of a romantic relationship with her. The officer suspected that she was the official's girlfriend and that this man may have arranged the marriage, so that she could get her paper to be legal in the U.S.

I could write an entire book filled with example after example about why you shouldn't hide information or lie to the immigration authorities. It is very likely that you are going to be found out. The odds are against you that you are going to get away with it. Mostly likely, you will get caught.

It's sad to see when this happens to my clients, or to individuals who handled their case without an attorney. The reason that I say it is sad is this: Had they told the truth instead of fabricating or hiding information, nothing would have happened to them. They simply would have been questioned about the facts, and the application or the case would have gone through without any consequence. By committing fraud, they got themselves into a situation that they could have avoided by telling the truth.

The Consequences of Lying or Concealing Information Marriage fraud.

If Immigration determines that you have committed marriage fraud (i.e., that you have used the immigration system to try to obtain a legal status through marriage), the laws are very clear about the consequences. You are permanently barred from ever obtaining any benefit from the government—even if you ever get married again. There are almost no exceptions to this rule.

This is why I always advise my clients to never do this. Whenever people come into my office and I detect that their case is based on fraud, I immediately advise them never to do that, because the consequences are so severe. I refuse their case. I want no part in fraud.

Inadmissibility.

Another consequence of fraud in the immigration system is that you will not be admissible. Inadmissibility means that you will not be allowed to enter the United States. That may seem strange to some folks because they are already in the United States, but the term inadmissibility means that the U.S. government is not going to give you any status that will allow you to become legal in the United States.

Denial of Application or Petition.

There is a natural consequence of getting caught committing fraud in the immigration system. Whatever application or petition that you filed will almost certainly be denied. On rare occasions, they may provide you with an opportunity to file for a waiver, but that is the exception to the rule. A waiver is a kind of forgiveness: If the waiver is granted, the law that would punish you for the fraud (or the reason for the waiver) is not applied to you. You are forgiven for the act. But most of the time, the application is simply denied. And in many instances, removal (deportation) proceedings are commenced.

Even if you are already being accused of fraud, there may be ways to avoid the consequence of a denial. For this to happen, you must speak to an experienced immigration attorney to see if you may qualify for certain waivers. These waivers are extremely complex and costly to prepare. A seasoned immigration lawyer can prepare one for you, but you need to know that there is no guarantee that the waiver will be granted. The best way to avoid having to file a waiver is to avoid the fraud or deception from the start.

Denial after the Fact.

The best way to explain this consequence is with an example of a client who recently came in to see me. He had been a legal resident for over 20 years. He obtained his permanent residency status by marrying a U.S. citizen two decades ago. What prompted the immigration officer to investigate deeper into his case was his recent application for naturalization. At the interview, the officer started asking him a whole bunch of questions about his marriage to his former wife.

Apparently during the application for citizenship, this officer discovered that he had fathered a child during the same time that he applied for his legal permanent-resident status via his former wife. In other words, he applied for the application, he went to an interview, he received his green card, and his paramour gave birth to his child out of wedlock—all within months of each other. He had to explain how he was married to a U.S. citizen wife while he had a relationship and fathered a child with another woman.

To top it all off, he divorced his wife within two months of obtaining his permanent-resident status and of the birth of his son. Of course, you have already figure out that it was suspected that he'd committed fraud 20 years earlier. Can you imagine how shocked he was when he was told that the immigration authorities were going to begin a deportation process to take back his permanent-resident status for committing fraud two decades ago?

Yes, that is correct. Immigration can take back anything they gave you. If fraud is ever discovered—even 20, 40, or 60 years later—they can undo whatever they did. This is how immigration authorities are able to take back citizenship and permanent-resident status from people who were found to have lied at some point in the process.

Some notorious examples are the cases of Nazi soldiers who were discovered in the United States, living comfortably in their retirement with U.S. citizenship. The government was able to prove fraud in their decades-old applications, when they were asked if they had ever been part of the Nazi Party. The proof was presented, and denaturalization processes were begun. Deportation followed, and they faced their accuser in their country of origin.

Summary

When dealing with immigration authorities—whether before a judge in an immigration court or with an officer for some other immigration agency—always tell the truth. Don't make things up, don't hide facts, and don't think that they are not going to find out the truth. Even innocent memory loss can be detrimental to your application or petition. My best piece of advice is that if you have any kind of doubt about anything you may be doing with an application or petition being presented to the government, always seek a legal opinion from an experienced attorney. Avoiding problems ahead of time is the smartest thing you can do.

Chapter 5:
Affidavit of Support Errors

"Numbers rule the universe."

- **Pythagoras (582 B.C. – about 507 B.C.)**

With few exceptions, almost every petition for a family member requires filing an Affidavit of Support with the application. This form is known as the I-864. The form was recently updated by USCIS, and as you can imagine, it didn't get any easier to fill out.

The purpose of the form is based on the general concept that a person immigrating to the United States on the petition of a family member should not become a charge (i.e., an expense) to the government. The family member needs to fill out this form and show that they have sufficient income and/or sufficient assets to support the person immigrating to the United States, based on the Federal Poverty Guidelines for the current year. (They change every year.)

In order for the visa to be issued or the change of status granted, the consul or immigration officer must see evidence (along with the Affidavit of Support) showing that the person coming into the U.S. is not going to be a charge to the government. This is a required application because U.S. law requires that no visa should be issued to any person who is likely to become a public charge.

The first mistake that people make when filling out their own paperwork during their petitions or applications is forgetting to include the I-864. Although this mistake is not always fatal to the application, it can cause delays in the process—sometimes for many, many months. But it is occasionally fatal.

I have many individuals come in to consult with me after the visa petition was denied for a family member living outside of the U.S. After investigating the case further, I find out that the reason for the denial was that the Affidavit of Support required by the embassy was incorrectly filled out, or it did not meet the requirements to show that the family would not be a charge to the government. Had they done it right the first time or had an attorney help them with it, they would have avoided the problem, stress, aggravation, and heartache of a denial.

The second biggest mistake that people make when filling out this form is submitting it with unqualified income. This means that their income does not meet the Federal Poverty Guidelines to show that they will be able to support the person getting the visa or legal permanent resident status. Whenever I prepare an Affidavit of Support, I always confirm that the listed income of the person signing the support is more than what the guidelines require. The accuracy of these numbers on the Affidavit is vital to the application, and you need to be sure it is filled out correctly.

When an Affidavit of Support is required, one of the biggest problems I have is that the person filing the petition does not have enough income to qualify for the application to be granted. Under the rules, they can still look for someone else to serve as a cosponsor to the beneficiary of the visa. Finding someone who is willing to fill out the Affidavit of Support as a cosponsor is not always easy—especially when they find out exactly what they are committing themselves to by doing so.

Anyone who fills out the Affidavit of Support and signs it, either as the main sponsor or a co-sponsor, is essentially giving assurances to the government that the beneficiary of the visa or change of status is not going to become a charge to the state (i.e., the government). Should that beneficiary receive any benefits from the government, they are also guaranteeing by signing the Affidavit that they will reimburse the government for the costs that were incurred.

There are different ways that the promises given in the Affidavit can be enforced by the government—or even by the person who received the visa or change of status. For example, when a U.S. citizen petitions for her husband, she has to sign an Affidavit of Support. Let's assume that a year and a half later, they separate, and the husband is unable to obtain work for some reason. Or the work that he does obtain is not enough for him to live on. Given that scenario, the wife will be responsible for spousal support, based on the Affidavit that she signed and filed with the immigration authorities. Now let's assume that they divorce. Even given that scenario, the ex-wife may be responsible for providing financial support to her husband, should he not be able to obtain work.

One big myth is that the Affidavit of Support expires after a certain period of time. This isn't exactly correct. An Affidavit of Support indefinitely obligates the person signing it, as long as the person receiving the visa is not a U.S. Citizen. There are some exceptions to this, but this is the reality in almost all cases.

Making Sure You do It Right

When there is a need to file an Affidavit of Support with an application, you must file one as the petitioner. This is the case, even if the petitioner has zero income. You then file the Affidavit reflecting the zero income of the petitioner. Next you prepare and file the Affidavit for the cosponsor, along with the first Affidavit.

Each person filing an Affidavit must include three main things with it:

1. **Proof of their legal status in the U.S.** This can be done with a U.S. birth certificate, a naturalization certificate, a U.S. passport, or a copy of their Legal Permanent Resident Card.

2. **A copy of their federal income tax form for the most recent year.** I now require tax transcripts, which the person can get directly from the Internal Revenue Service.

3. If the person is employed, I always include **a letter from their employer**, confirming their employment, position or job title, and income. If they are self-employed, I ask for the latest Income and Expense Statement from their business.

All this is included with the filed I-864 Affidavit when the primary application is filed. There is a way to file an Affidavit when a person is living off of their assets. In those cases, I strongly recommend that the person get an experienced immigration lawyer to make sure that the

Affidavit, along with all the proper evidence, is prepared correctly.

Summary

To avoid mistakes with the Affidavit, you should always make sure you do the following:

- Know when to file it (and when not to).

- Know what forms and supporting documents need to be filed along with the Affidavit of Support.

- Avoid delays by making sure that the person signing the Affidavit of Support has enough income to qualify them to meet the Federal Poverty Guidelines.

- Make sure that you fill out the form correctly and completely.

Don't forget to sign it.

Chapter 6:
Interview Errors

"Smart people learn from their mistakes. But the real sharp ones learn from the mistakes of others."

- **Brandon Mull,** *Fablehaven*

The day of your interview has come. You're all nervous. The stress and tension levels are high. Are you ready for this? Do you have everything you need? Do you know what you're doing? Have you been properly prepared for what to expect?

The number of mistakes that I have had to fix for clients because they went to their interviews unprepared is incalculable.

One obvious mistake is missing an interview. This can happen for different reasons. Maybe your nerves got the best of you, and you did not go out of fear. Maybe you forgot to send USCIS a change of address. Maybe your mail didn't make it to you. There are different ways to make sure that you are notified of all interview dates. One of the best ways is to have an attorney, who will get a copy of everything that you need, including hearing dates. Obviously, the most likely consequences of missing a hearing are that the application or petition will be denied. With the help of an attorney, there may be ways to reverse this.

Another common mistake is forgetting important documents. On the hearing notice from USCIS, there is always a list of important documents that need to be brought to the appointment. When I represent someone that has an interview, I sit down with them a few days before we go, and I review everything that is going to happen at the interview. I remind them of all the documents that they need to take with them. Even with this preparation, I have had clients forget documents. One time, a couple I represented just showed up and didn't bring anything with them. As you can imagine, their case didn't go so well.

Whenever I prepare any of my clients for testifying—whether it would be in court or at a USCIS interview—I always give them an example of how to answer a question by showing them a pen. I ask them, "What is this?" Most of the time, I get a simple answer: "It's a pen." And then I say, "Exactly." No one asked them for any specific information, other than to say what it was they were being shown. I didn't ask about brand, type, size, shell color, ink color, or anything else. I only asked them to tell me what it was. This is good advice for any type of hearing or interview, regardless of the setting—whether it be criminal, immigration, or civil. <u>Answer only what you are asked</u>.

So another common mistake is talking too much. Because they were nervous, I've had clients who began talking too much, and they did not stick to just answering the question that was asked. In one case, my client kept talking and talking so much, I started trying to kick her under the table to signal her to shut up. Talking too much can sometimes open up a can worms during the questioning. This has happened to so many of my clients, even after preparing them in my office. Please remember: listen to the questions, and answer only the questions.

Don't embellish or ramble on, unless it is absolutely necessary (which it normally isn't).

Similar to the first mistake about forgetting documents, **another mistake is taking the wrong documents to an interview**. Many folks also forget to take original documents with them, even though the interview notice reminded them to do so. In most interviews, the hearing officer may want to see original documents, such as birth certificates, marriage certificates, death certificates, and divorce decrees. The reason the officer needs to see these is to be able compare the original documents with any copies that were mailed with the application or petition. Forgetting documents, bringing the wrong documents, or not bringing original documents can cause delays in the processing of an application or petition. In some cases, it may even result in the denial of an application.

If the person being interviewed does not know English, they must bring an interpreter. Without an interpreter, your case could be delayed or even denied. In most hearing or interview notices, it clearly states that an interpreter needs to go with the person being interviewed if they do not know English. They *may* not need an interpreter because the officer speaks their language, but this isn't normally the case. The only time you are provided with an interpreter by the government is in an immigration court. For everything else, always take an interpreter with you, so that you'll have one there if you need one.

Next, **don't argue with the hearing officer**. You may have a good point. You may even be right when they're wrong. But most of the time, you are not going to get anywhere by arguing. <u>Don't argue with the hearing officer</u>. There are ways to get your point across. Rarely does arguing get you anywhere with hearing officers, judges, or anyone who has the authority to make a decision about your case or application.

Finally, **dress appropriately**. You are not going to a night club or a disco. This isn't your cousin's wedding. Dress in fine, casual, or conservative clothing. In this situation, dressing plainly is good. Don't put on anything too flashy. And for goodness' sake, leave all the jewelry at home, except for wedding rings and simple accessories. Remember: where you are going, perception is very important.

Chapter 7:
Not Knowing Your Status

"Knowing is half the battle."

- **Anthony J. D'Angelo**

Most of the time, people know what immigration status they have in the United States. This isn't always a very big problem, but it is a mistake that is seen often enough that it merits being put in this book. It is important to know what status you have in the United States. That way you'll know what you may or may not be able to do in the future, depending on your status.

Simply put, there are three categories that you can be in. You can be "in status," you can be "out of status," or you can have "no status." Let me explain exactly what each of those terms mean.

Being In Status

Generally speaking, being in status means that you have lawful permission to be in the United States. This could include anything from having legal permanent resident status, citizenship, or a visa entry that has not elapsed. It could also mean any other type of status that the immigration authorities have given you, which allows you to be in the United States for some purpose—and with some kind of legal status.

It could be a student visa, or you may have been granted asylum. It could be one of the many different types of work visas, or it could be an athlete's visa. You may have been allowed to enter the country to speak at a convention, or you may have been paroled into the country.

The point is that for whatever reason, you have some kind of legal status in the United States, and you are permitted to be here.

Being Out of Status

Out of status usually means that at some point, you had legal status, but you somehow lost it. A typical example is having a visa that allowed you to be in the United States for a specific period of time, and you have stayed longer than that time period. So by overstaying your visa, you are now out of status.

The situation could also be that you had legal permanent resident status at one point, but for some reason, you lost it. One example of how you can lose legal permanent residency status is by staying outside of the United States for more than one year, at which point it's considered that you have abandoned your legal permanent resident status.

Another way is by committing a crime and going through a removal process, in which a judge issues an order of removal (deportation) in your case. However, a person who is out of status usually came into the United States with a visa and overstayed.

Having No Status

A third category that sometimes gets mixed in with the category of "out of status" is having "no status." The typical example of a person who has no status is someone who enters the United States without being inspected. That is legal jargon that means that they somehow entered illegally. Some examples of illegal entries include the classic crossing the border without permission, entering the United States with fake papers, or traveling as a stowaway on an airplane, ship, or some other vessel.

But when you think about it, even a person who has "no status" actually has the status I just mentioned, otherwise known as "entered without inspection" (EWI). So remember this if you entered the U.S. illegally (without legal authorization to be in the U.S.), and you are filling out an immigration application: When you get to the question where they ask for your status, make sure you put down EWI.

What You Can Do, Depending on Your Status

Why is it important to know what your status is? The simple answer is because what your status is now may affect what you can or cannot do in the United States once an application or petition is filed.

For example, a U.S. citizen can petition for every type of immediate family that he or she has. A legal permanent resident cannot petition for every type of immediate family. If you are an overstay (out of status) in the United

States, you may be able to adjust your status in certain conditions. However, if you are a person who has no status (EWI), you may not be able to adjust your status in the U.S., and you would have to leave the U.S. to pick up a visa in the consulate in your country. But there may be exceptions to this.

Do you see how confusing it can get? That's why having a good, experienced immigration attorney by your side is essential to work through all of the confusion and know exactly what you can or cannot do.

Another important reason to know your status is that there are consequences that can occur, based on your status. As an example, imagine that a person has no status, which means that they entered the U.S. by crossing a border without inspection. If for any reason this person leaves the borders of the United States—even for an instant—there is a law that is automatically triggered. That means that a certain law automatically applies to them, simply because they stepped foot outside of the United States.

This particular law says that if they have been in the United States for six months—but less than one year—and traveled outside of the United States, they are now barred from receiving any benefit or from coming back into the United States for three years. They physically have to stay outside of the United States for three years, before they can come back in legally. If they have been in the United States for over one year—and that means even one day over a year—then that punishment goes up to 10 years. They have to physically remain outside of the United States for 10 years, before they can get any benefit from the government immigration authorities.

A sad example of how that applies involves a recent client of mine, who was in the United States with Temporary Protection Status (TPS.) She had been here for many years. She still has two minor children in the United States. She was given enough warning to apply for an advanced parole. This is a permission to reenter the United States after traveling outside of it, without having the 3 or 10-year bar applied to you.

However, she made a grave mistake. She didn't use the advanced parole on time. She suddenly found herself having to travel back to her country because of a death in her family. She thought that the advanced parole was going to help her, except that it had expired. That advanced parole would have protected her from the 10-year bar, which would have applied to her leaving the United States. In other words, she would have been able to travel outside the United States and return without that punishment being applied to her.

But because she traveled outside of the United States with an <u>expired</u> parole, it did not protect her. She found herself in her country of origin, unable to travel back to the United States with two minor children waiting for her. Having the TPS did not help her case. The consulate in her country did not and could not help her. She was prevented from reentering the U.S. after traveling abroad. She broke the law, and the consequences were severe.

Another example of the importance of knowing your status is a different case I had. A young man in his early 20s was detained by Immigration and Customs Enforcement (I.C.E.) for committing a crime. He had been a legal permanent resident in the U.S. since he was a child, just like his entire family had been. They all entered the U.S. together. His mother and father both became U.S. citizens several years prior to that, when he was still a teenager. This young man was detained by I.C.E. for several months before his family called me.

Immediately after reviewing his case, I was able to determine that he was in fact already a U.S. citizen. You see, when his parents became U.S. citizens while he was still a teenager, he automatically became a U.S. citizen, along with his parents—by operation of the law. He derived his citizenship from his parents. I immediately filed a motion to terminate proceedings, and he was released right away.

Summary

If you don't know what your status is or what you can do with the status you do have, go see a good, experienced lawyer to get a full, deep understanding of what's involved. As you can see from the examples I gave in this chapter, there may be ways for you to benefit from knowing your status, or there may be ways to avoid trouble by finding out.

Chapter 8:
The Consequences of
Having a Criminal Record

*"Crime has always been a regrettably consistent element
of the human experience."*

- **Mark Frost, *The List of Seven***

Any immigrant in the United States—whether they are
here either legally (with status of some kind) or illegally
(either out of status or with no status)—may face certain
consequences if they have any kind of criminal conviction.
Note that I said conviction. This is because being arrested
alone—without a conviction—might not have
consequences regarding immigration. However, the
consequences can be detrimental, depending on the type
of criminal conviction that someone has in their history.

If you have any kind of criminal history, my best advice to
you is to seek out an experienced immigration lawyer, and
have an in-depth consultation with them. That way, the
attorney can determine what kind of impact this criminal
history will have on your case. Anything less would be an
extremely bad idea, given the fact that the consequences
for a conviction can be so severe.

Even if there was an arrest but the case ended without a
conviction, you could still have serious problems.
Sometimes, an arrest alone could greatly affect the
possibility of receiving a favorable decision from
immigration authorities. The mere fact that you may have

participated in a criminal act may prevent you from being eligible for immigration benefits, such as a visa, legal permanent resident status, or U.S. citizenship.

What is "Reason to Believe?"

I had a client who was an older man when he came to the U.S. from Cuba. He entered the U.S. with a parole status.

A few months after he arrived in the U.S., he saw an old friend on the street, so he stopped to pick him up. A few blocks later, the police stopped the car and arrested both of them on drug-trafficking charges. It seems that this old friend was being watched by the police. And precisely at the time my client picked him up—just to give him a ride somewhere—the police closed in on him and arrested him. They found large amounts of drugs on him, and my client was arrested as a suspected accomplice. Fortunately, my client's friend told the police the truth; my client was released, and the charges were dropped.

The following year, he applied for his green card. He was denied for something the immigration authorities call "reason to believe." That means that even though you have no conviction and the charges were dropped or dismissed, the government is saying that they have "reason to believe" that you still did it, and you got away with the crime with no conviction. What do you think about that? Sounds crazy, doesn't it? But that's the law.

Typical Mistakes About Criminal History

When thinking about criminal history and immigration, some common mistakes that people make include:

1.   Thinking that a misdemeanor is not a problem.

2.   Thinking that sealing a record or doing an expungement avoids a problem.

3.   Omitting information about criminal history in applications or petitions.

That last example could be considered immigration fraud, as discussed in a previous chapter of this book.

The Different Levels of Crimes

Anyone who has ever watched any detective or lawyer show on TV has a general idea of how the criminal system works, in both local courts and federal criminal courts. We all know that there are different levels of crimes—from low, summary offenses (e.g., for traffic violations) to high-felony crimes.

Usually, there are several layers of summary offenses. They are followed by several layers of misdemeanors, going from a Misdemeanor 3 to a Misdemeanor 2 to a Misdemeanor 1. Then those levels of crimes are followed by felony levels, such as a Felony 3 to a Felony 2 to a Felony 1. Those higher levels of crimes are usually then followed by the crimes that everyone knows are really bad—like murder, kidnaping, and rape. This concept of a pyramid of criminal levels is pretty much universally understood, with a few differences from state to state.

How the Immigration Law Looks at a Crime

However, according to the immigration laws, whatever crime is committed by a noncitizen is generally categorized in one of three levels. By that, I mean that the convictions received in a local court or federal court are interpreted by immigration laws as being in one of three different categories:

1. Crimes With No Immigration Consequences

The first category are crimes that have no consequences with immigration. There really is no official name for this level. The crimes that fit into this category are considered low-level offenses, such as running a red light, littering, or speeding. Having no consequences means that even if you have a conviction for this type of low-level crime, you will not be affected in almost any immigration proceeding.

Even though some crimes may not affect your ability to get a benefit from immigration, there are several crimes that fall into this category; they may affect the timespan in which you can obtain a benefit. One classic example is applying for naturalization. During the naturalization process, you have to prove that you have good moral character.

While not preventing you from applying for naturalization, certain crimes may eventually disallow you from obtaining your citizenship for a period of time (usually up to five years from the date of the conviction). For example, let's say the person applying for naturalization had a petty-theft crime within the last five years. Usually, having this type of crime on your record does not prevent you from applying for citizenship, but you have to wait until at least five years have passed from the time of the conviction for that crime—not from the time the crime was committed. After that five-year period, you should be able to apply for naturalization. (But remember, the "reason to believe" explanation given above.)

2. Crimes Involving Moral Turpitude

The next level of crimes are called crimes involving moral turpitude (CIMT.) As interpreted by immigration law, this level of crimes does prevent certain individuals from applying for certain benefits. In fact, committing a crime that is considered a CIMT can move a person who already has their legal permanent residence into a deportation proceeding. Immigration law makes a person who is a noncitizen convicted of a CIMT removable, if the crime was committed within five years from the date of their admission into the U.S.—and if it resulted in a sentence of imprisonment for at least one year. If a person is convicted of two CIMTs that did not arise out of a single incidence of criminal misconduct, they are also removable.

When determining whether a person has committed a crime that is considered a CIMT, there is also much more involved. This is a complex area of immigration law, which requires the assistance of an experienced immigration lawyer. Don't depend on your criminal lawyer for this analysis, unless they have extensive immigration law experience. They may be great criminal lawyers, but I've found that most criminal lawyers don't know much about immigration law—or the way criminal laws and immigration laws affect each other.

3. Crimes That Are Considered Aggravated Felonies

The final level of crimes actually has a title I don't like. The crimes that fall into this level are called "aggravated felonies." The reason I do not like that title is because in certain states, there are some *misdemeanor* crimes that fall into the category of aggravated felonies—from the immigration law perspective.

The consequence of having your conviction being considered an aggravated felony is fatal. This means that in an immigration removal proceeding, you are not eligible for bond if you are detained, and you most likely are not eligible for any kind of relief, except for withholding or removal. To clarify, "most likely" means there are just a few rare exceptions to this.

Once again, this book is not designed to go into a full explanation of the consequences of criminal convictions. The point I want to make is that there are serious consequences for crimes. Always consult with an immigration attorney if you believe you may fall into any one of the categories discussed here.

Other Errors to Avoid

If you have any kind of criminal conviction and you are a noncitizen in the U.S., you should always consult with an immigration attorney before you do any of the following:

1. Do Not Travel Outside of the U.S.

This includes even a one-day cruise or a day trip across the border. Many of my deportation clients become my clients because they took a trip out of the U.S. And when they came back, they were detained by Immigration and Customs Enforcement (ICE). Usually, what follows is the commencement of a deportation process against that person. In many cases, they are detained for weeks before they can be released on bond. In some cases, they are not eligible for bond, and they must remain detained while I fight their deportation case.

2. Do Not Submit Any Application or Benefit with USCIS.

Sometimes, trouble for a client starts because they submitted an application for a benefit with the government, and they have a criminal conviction on their record. As part of processing some of these applications, background checks are done. If it is discovered that the person has a crime on their record, they may wind up in a deportation proceeding.

3. Do Not Commit Another Crime.

Even a simple, low-level crime can blow up in your face if you are a noncitizen with a previous criminal history. This seems logical, but some people don't realize the consequences of their actions until it's too late. They figure that the last time they got in trouble, nothing happened with the immigration authorities. So why now? They learn the hard way that their luck has run out.

Some of my clients thought they had "gotten away" with several crimes because action was not taken by the immigration authorities. Then they get in trouble for simple things like traffic infractions. That's when they get detained, and their immigration nightmares begin.

Defending Against Deportation

An entire book can be written just on this topic alone. As I said before, this book is not written to discuss immigration laws. Instead, it is designed to educate you about things you can do to avoid problems. There might be ways to defend against deportation. But for that to happen, you need to have a detailed consultation with an attorney, who can review your criminal history. Then you can see if you qualify for any of the forms of defense against being removed back to your country. My best advice is to do this before you ever find yourself in the hands of the government.

Summary

The consequences of having a criminal conviction if you are a noncitizen can be fatal to your ability to get a benefit from the immigration authorities, or to keep your legal permanent resident status. This part of immigration law is one of the most complex areas. Without question, this is an area of the law that requires consulting a good immigration attorney. Only then can you make sure that you have all the information you need, in order to know whether there is something that can be done about your case.

If you have a criminal conviction and you have immigration proceedings commenced against you, there may be ways to avoid removal or deportation. But as I said above, you must discuss this with an attorney. This is definitely one thing that you cannot do yourself—or have done by people who are not licensed professionals.

Chapter 9:
Marriage Application
Problems (Fraud and
Other Issues)

*"A successful marriage requires falling in love many
times, always with the same person."*

- **Mignon McLaughlin**

Fraud

Within the immigration system, one of the most carefully
scrutinized applications is for legal permanent resident
status through marriage. The reason for this is that
marriage is the #1 way that fraud is committed within the
immigration system.

Marriage fraud is the filing of an application based on a
marriage to a U.S. citizen or legal permanent resident—
when that marriage is not real. Having a marriage
certificate does not make a marriage real; it makes it legal,
but not real. I cannot believe how many people still try this
as a way to obtain their legal permanent resident status.
Trying to fool immigration through a sham marriage (as it
is usually called) is one of the most foolish things that a
person can do.

Whenever I find out that a potential client is trying to
commit marriage fraud, the first thing I tell them is that I

will not be any part of it. I have even been known to abruptly show them the door to my office, because I am so against this type of activity. The consequences are extremely severe for anyone who is caught participating. An attorney who participates in this type of fraud would likely lose their license. My professional reputation and license are not worth participating in a criminal act.

Marriage fraud is a federal crime, which can result in a prison sentence—and almost certainly the deportation of the person attempting it. If the spouse who is already a U.S. citizen or a legal permanent resident is found to have committed this fraud after filing a petition, he or she would be in jeopardy of severe punishments. And it is almost certain that the person applying for the benefit would not get it, and he or she would forever be prevented from applying for any benefit in the future ever again. This includes filing for legal permanent resident status—even if they ever remarry, and this marriage is genuine.

Getting Married Too Soon After Coming to the U.S.

Another very common mistake that some people make is getting married too soon after they enter the United States. Let me explain. Some people come into the U.S. with a fiancé visa, which is intended for them to enter the country and get married here. Other people enter the U.S. with other types of visas. The most typical visa is a tourist or visitor's visa.

When you enter as a tourist, visitor, or student (or under any other type of visa), you are representing to the government that your intention in the U.S. is to do what they issued the visa to do. Did you enter with a tourist visa? Be a tourist. Go here, there, and everywhere, but do not work. Did you come here to study with a student visa? Study to your heart's content, but that is all you can do.

Some immigrants—who have managed to enter the U.S. on a tourist, visitor, or student visa—get married after entering. The immigration laws may look at this as visa fraud. They may say that when you came into the U.S., your real intention was not to be a tourist; rather, it was actually to stay and get married. There is a presumption in the law: If you get married within the first 60 days of your entry into the U.S., then that is evidence that your intention all along was really to get married—and not for the purpose of the visa you were issued.

To overcome that presumption, the immigrant needs to prove that he or she did not commit visa fraud by misusing the visa. They have to show that when they entered the U.S., their real intention at all times was not to stay, get married, and get a U.S. green card. It would be fine if the person can prove that they really came as a tourist (for vacation, etc.), and then they met their spouse later on. In order to avoid this presumption, the longer the time period between the entry into the U.S. and the submission of the green card application, the better.

Do It Right the First Time

For permanent resident status by way of marriage to a U.S. citizen or legal permanent resident, it is very important that the applications (and all the related paperwork) be done absolutely correctly. You do not want to give the immigration officer any reason to suspect your application, reject it, or (worse yet) determine that there is marriage fraud in the application. Don't be fooled into thinking that just because the marriage is real, they cannot deem the marriage a fraud.

There are so many times that I've had clients that did all the paperwork on their own, or they went through a notario office or one of those "fly-by-night" outfits that only fill out the paperwork. Because the work was so poorly done, the immigration officer denied the application—and in many cases, even accused the couple of marriage fraud.

To minimize any chance of finding yourself in trouble that results in very severe repercussions, you want to make sure that this type of application—or any other type of application, for that matter—is done absolutely correctly. Remember that the government looks at every case very closely, including what may seem like a very simple case. You don't want to give the government any reason to reject your application.

Don't Underestimate the Process

The typical mistake that genuine married couples make is underestimating the process for this type of application. They naively think that just because they are genuinely in love, somehow the immigration officer is going to know that; they're going to see the aura of love around them and automatically approve their application. In many cases, this could not be further from the truth.

When I am preparing my clients for their case—especially for their interview with USCIS—I always tell them that we have to go into that interview assuming that the officer is conducting it with the purpose of finding fraud in the application. It is our job to convince the officer that this is in fact a genuine, bona fide marriage. I always extensively prepare my clients for any interview with practice questions and examples of what to say and not say. I never want my clients to underestimate the process, even if they have children as evidence of their genuine marriage.

Getting Your Marriage Application Granted

The best way to win your marriage application case is to prepare, prepare, prepare. The person conducting the interview doesn't know you at all. You have to convince them that the marriage is genuine, and that you are living together. By the way, this is another mistake that people make in applications based on marriage: They think that a marriage certificate is all they need, even if they are now separated.

Part of the requirement when granting the application is that the couple must still be living together. You have to present evidence of the fact that the marriage is real AND that you are still together. As I prepare my clients for the part of the process when we combine the application with the evidence, I tell them that the less of a traditional marriage they have, the more likely it is that they are going to have trouble with their application.

Let me explain what I mean by that: The immigration laws regarding the requirements for a marriage application were written many decades ago. They were not written with our modern society in mind. In the days that these laws were written, couples would get married and immediately start commingling everything together. Couples would get mutual bank accounts, put everything in both names, and include each other in all legally required paperwork. In our modern society, couples get separate bank accounts, and they separate ownership of property. And they do many other things in their own names, without including the other half of the couple.

The more the application looks like the old-fashioned way of doing things, the more likely it is that the application is going to get approved. Conversely, the more it looks like a modern couple's way of doing things, the more probable it is that all kinds of things are going to be questioned. This is simply a reality we have to live with. I'm not saying a "modern" couple won't get approved. What I am saying is that the modern couple is more likely to have problems with their application.

What Evidence to Submit

The type of evidence that needs to be submitted for this type of application includes the traditional things that everyone thinks about: pictures, joint bank accounts, other types of accounts, joint ownership of both real and personal property, leases for real estate in joint names, and any other evidence that shows commingling.

When I prepare my couples for their application, I ask them to think about every type of evidence that can be used to show that they are in fact a genuine couple living together. Of course, statements or affidavits from landlords, neighbors, and family members help a lot. If either party has children from prior marriages who are in school, getting school documentation showing that the other spouse is listed as an authorized guardian of the child also helps a lot. The list is endless.

I show my clients the details that we are trying to prove in the application. I prepare their applications meticulously, with the goal of having everything included. That way, the reviewing officer sees all the evidence I submit, and he or she will be inclined to approve the application without an interview. Of course, this doesn't always happen, but preparing an application as completely as possible increases the chances.

Summary

The importance of getting professional help when doing a marriage application cannot be overstated. Knowing how to prepare for your application is very important. Obtaining sufficient evidence to prove that the marriage is real is critical to having the application approved without a problem. Prepare, prepare, prepare. Don't underestimate the process. In this area of immigration law, that is the most likely, biggest mistake you can make.

Chapter 10:
Tax Return Filings

"Income tax returns are the most imaginative fiction being written today."

- **Herman Wouk**

You may be wondering what tax returns have to do with any type of immigration process. But it is important to know that the proper filing of tax returns is critical to many immigration petitions, applica3tions, and certain types of deportation case defenses.

Naturalization Cases

Here's one example of why it is important to properly file tax returns: In order to be able to apply for naturalization, you must have filed tax returns. If you have not filed tax returns (or if you owe a debt to the Internal Revenue Service, which you have not made arrangements to pay), it is very likely that your naturalization application will be denied.

Most people mostly worry about the portion of the naturalization process that involves an English test, but that is only a small percentage of what is reviewed in the entire application. Making sure that you have properly filed tax returns is essential to having your naturalization application granted.

57

Marriage Applications

Having a properly filed tax return is also vitally important when applying for a benefit via marriage to a U.S. citizen or a legal permanent resident. Remember that you have to show that the relationship is genuine and bona fide, and every area of your life can be explored by an immigration officer to confirm that. Many people who fill out these applications on their own fail to consider their tax returns as part of that evidence.

When filing tax returns, you can either file as single, married filing jointly, married filing separately, or head of household. That last category is the one that gets most people in trouble. This is because they file as head of household to get benefits that they may not be entitled to receive if they file any other way. With few exceptions, if you are married and living together, you must file either married filing jointly or married filing separately. You normally cannot file as head of household.

Incorrect Filing Status

In an immigration context, a typical example of this becoming a problem is a situation such as a husband and wife living together with at least one child. By filing jointly or separately but under the category of married, they may not be entitled to certain benefits offered to people who would file as head of household.

Despite the fact that they are not eligible to file as head of household, they do anyway. From a tax revenue office's perspective, this is fraud. Not only can this be used against the couple if they are trying to convince a judge or immigration officer reviewing their case that their marriage is genuine. The logic is that if they are genuinely married and living together, they would need to file something other than head of household. Keep in mind that filing fraudulent tax returns can be viewed as proving bad moral character, and it can cause the denial of certain types of applications.

Tax Returns and Deportation Cases

Properly filing tax returns is also very important if you are in front of an immigration court during deportation proceedings. Numerous times, I have seen judges react favorably and congratulate individuals for the following reason: Despite lacking proper authorization in the United States, they had the presence of mind to obtain an individual tax identification number (ITIN) from the IRS, and they used it to file tax returns every year that they worked here. This is very favorable for certain types of waivers, as well as other types of immigration applications.

Conversely, I have also seen judges chastise people. They consider it very unfavorable that people who have lived here for many years have never filed tax returns, despite having worked here. Anyone reading this has to know that if you work in the United States—regardless of the type of work you do—you have to file tax returns. That includes legal or illegal work. Al Capone, the famous gangster from the 1930s, was not arrested and jailed for all of the violent crimes that he was famous for. He was put in jail for tax evasion. He failed to pay taxes on the income he made from his illegal business.

Getting an Individual Tax Identification Number (ITIN)

Getting an ITIN is not difficult, and the IRS will give you one, even if you are illegally in the U.S. You can get one online at the IRS website, or by mailing a form to the IRS and requesting one. The IRS is not in the business of reporting people who are in the U.S. illegally to the ICE or any other immigration agency. Their goal is to get people to file returns and pay their taxes. Getting a reputation for turning people over to the immigration authorities defeats this purpose, so they don't do it.

Getting IRS Transcripts

I am now recommending to all of my clients that they immediately obtain tax transcripts from the IRS, and that they keep copies of these transcripts with them. Then they'll have them available at all times. The reason why is because across the board, immigration authorities are now looking to obtain tax return transcripts—rather than just copies of returns when considering applications that they are processing. The transcripts prove that you actually filed the returns with the IRS, while the copies of the returns only show that you filled out the forms.

Improperly Claiming Dependents on Tax Returns

Another common mistake people filing tax returns make is claiming children or other individuals as dependents on their tax returns, who they cannot legally claim. With very few exceptions, you can only claim children who either live with you, who are in the United States, or who you somehow have the legal right to claim on tax returns. If you claim a child who does not live with you on your returns, you need a signed IRS form from the other parent, or a copy of a custody agreement showing that you are allowed to claim the child.

When it comes to properly filing tax returns, my best advice is to consult a professional. Go to a Certified Public Accountant (CPA) or another experienced, reputable person. Don't go to the cheapest place or to an office where they will incorrectly or fraudulently fill out your returns. The consequence will not only be financially disastrous; doing so could also adversely affect your immigration status or application possibilities.

Summary

Filing tax returns properly is a very important part of the immigration process. As an immigration attorney, I am not trying to give tax advice. There are numerous professionals for that. My only advice is this: Seek professional, ethical advice when filling out tax returns. So many immigrants in the United States go to fly-by-night offices, where people pretend to know what they are doing with tax returns. But in reality, they only get filers into serious trouble, which can affect them both financially and, as explained above, in their immigration process.

Make sure you file under the right status. Also make sure that you do indeed file your tax returns. And don't forget to always keep copies of whatever you file.

Chapter 11:
Marriage Application Errors

"I love being married. It's so great to find that one special person you want to annoy for the rest of your life."

-     **Rita Rudner**

Now you understand the dangers of trying to fraudulently apply for a benefit through marriage. And when there is in fact a genuine marriage, you know the importance of filling out an application correctly. At this point, let me show you some examples of the common mistakes that people make when filing their applications based on marriage.

First, you have to understand that the approval of an application is not guaranteed. In addition to proving that the marriage is genuine (and not a sham), you have to prove that you legally qualify for a benefit, based on a marriage to a U.S. citizen or a legal permanent resident.

Are You Really Married?

The first thing I do when I take on a case involving a marriage application is to determine whether or not the couple I am helping is actually married. Believe it or not, people have come into my office thinking that they have

63

been married for years. Then after I dig deeper into their case, I discover that they in fact have not ever been legally married, or that their marriage is not recognized by U.S. immigration law. (And no, it is not bigamy unless it was entered into knowing that they were still married. Usually, some form of deception is involved for it to be bigamy.)

In one case of mine, the couple had been living together for over 20 years, thinking they were married that whole time. They had children, property, and all the typical things that married couples have. When they came in to see me, I discovered that the husband had a previous marriage in his country. He thought he had obtained a divorce from his previous wife, but there was no divorce to be found.

He explained to me that his ex-wife told him that she had filed a divorce. Indeed, she had also "remarried." For him, that was enough. But unfortunately, it wasn't in the eyes of the law. He was still married to his first wife, and his marriage to his second wife was actually not a marriage at all—because he was not legally able to remarry.

The good thing is that they came to see me before they did any paperwork, and we were able to fix the problem by having a divorce from the first wife processed. Then he was able to remarry his second wife. After that, we were able to submit all the proper paperwork. At the interview with the immigration officer several months later, I appeared with them and was able to explain everything. Their application was subsequently approved.

Unacceptable Marriages

In another case, the couple had a marriage certificate. They did the paperwork through a notary office, and it was accepted as genuine. And in fact, it was genuine. However,

64

the marriage was done through what is called a power of attorney. That means that one party was not physically present during the ceremony, and he gave someone else the power of attorney to sit in for them at the ceremony. In this case, my client was not even in the country when he married his wife.

While that type of marriage may be considered legitimate and permissible in the country where this ceremony occurred, U.S. immigration law does not generally recognize such a marriage for the purposes of an immigration process. Sadly, their application was denied because Immigration did not recognize the marriage. Therefore, the application had no validity.

The stress, aggravation, and cost they incurred could have been avoided, had they gone to see someone who knew what they were doing—instead of an office that simply filled out the paperwork and pretended to know how to do it. Again, almost anyone can fill out an application. Knowing how to put together a properly supported package takes experience, as well as a good understanding of the law.

Don't Make Plans Until the Paper is in Your Hand

Another common mistake is assuming that the process is going to occur quickly. Most people don't really know how long it's going to take. Whenever I get asked that question (and I get asked by almost every client), I answer by telling them the average amount of time that their type of case takes.

I always caution them that with any immigration process or case, we can only predict a general idea of how long it is going to take. No one can ever be certain, because there are always situations when the case may take much longer than anticipated. There could be many reasons for this happening.

I counsel my clients to not make any plans or spend any money on anything that has a deadline or is time-sensitive—until they actually have the documents in their hands. Only then can they know for certain that they have received the benefit that they have asked the government for.

Summary

These are the common errors to avoid when filing a marriage-based application for legal permanent residency status:

1. Make sure you are legally married.
2. Make sure that you have been divorced from any previous marriage.
3. Make sure that your marriage is recognized by U.S. immigration laws.
4. Don't assume that the process is going to be quick.
5. Don't make plans that are based on the assumption that the process will take a specific time.

Chapter 12:
Other Typical Mistakes to Avoid

"A smart man makes a mistake, learns from it, and never makes that mistake again. But a wise man finds a smart man and learns from him how to avoid the mistake altogether."

- **Roy H. Williams**

In previous chapters, I have tried to identify and explain some of the biggest mistakes that are made when dealing with the immigration system. Below are a few others. These errors are seen often, and they should be avoided. Some are small, and some are big. Any of them can destroy a person's case.

1. Asking for Legal Advice from Government Offices

You need to know that USCIS and other immigration agencies or offices are not allowed to give you any type of legal advice. It is a huge mistake to think that they can. They can give you some procedural advice, but that is about all they can or should do.

I have had numerous clients who were given some guidance by an employee in a government office, which was actually bad advice for their specific case. They do not do it on purpose; they just don't have enough information.

Giving good, sound legal advice requires consulting with the person to get all the facts before dispensing it. One slight change in facts in a specific case can make the difference between filing one thing or filing another thing. And it can make the difference between success and failure.

2. Leaving the U.S. or Traveling

I strongly suggest that you always talk to an experienced immigration attorney before you do any kind of traveling outside of the United States. This is especially true if you have any kind of criminal history, or if you have no current status in the U.S.

Traveling outside of the United States can have severe consequences on your immigration status or your ability to file for something in the future. You can lose a benefit you have gotten, you could be prevented from reentering the U.S., or you can be detained and put into a deportation proceeding upon arriving back in the U.S.

Do not travel before you speak to an immigration attorney that can review your specific case and let you know if it is okay. Avoid cruises, or even just fishing near international borders. In coastal states, it's not uncommon for the Coast Guard to find a boat in international waters with someone on board that has no status in the U.S., or with a criminal history that makes them deportable or inadmissible. Be very careful.

3. Listening to Street Lawyers

These are people who have the "I know it all" syndrome, but they only give bad advice. They have no legal education, but they think they know the law. They may even sound convincing. Their "legal advice" is dangerous, and it can significantly affect the case of the person listening to that advice. Over the years, I have had very sad cases; because individuals listened to street lawyers or people who thought they knew what they were talking about, they followed their advice and lost an opportunity to apply for a benefit for them and/or their family.

If you are going to listen to anyone at all, make sure it is an experienced immigration attorney. My mother always told me that cheap things turn out expensive in the end. Listening to free legal advice from "street lawyers" is not only foolish, it can turn out to be an expensive and tragic mistake.

4. Not Financially Planning for the Inevitable

I once had a client in a drug case that was well-prepared for what he saw as the inevitable. He knew that sooner or later, he was going to be arrested. He was prepared. The day he was arrested, he had the funds saved up to pay for his lawyer, and for the very high bail amount that was set in his case. There was no financial stress on his family, or the typical running around for money to get him out. He had good, quick representation for his criminal case.

I believe doing the same for an immigration case is what everyone with a potential case should do. Are you here illegally? Then you should prepare for the day you get detained by the government. Do you have a criminal case that can have immigration consequences? Be prepared for it. Are you able to apply for naturalization soon? Save up for the filing fees.

Don't get caught unprepared. There's no reason to stress out your loved ones by not planning ahead.

5. Not Filing for a Benefit on Time

This is worth repeating: It is important to make sure you file an application on time. If you are filing to renew or extend a benefit you have, don't miss a deadline. Knowing what to file and filing in a timely manner will avoid the possibility of losing your status or ending up in the country illegally. You want to apply as early as possible because the applications can take several months to be processed. Don't wait until the very last minute.

6. Participating in Immigration Scams

There is an old saying that if it seems too good to be true, it probably is. I am heartbroken every time someone comes into my office and tells me about how they were scammed by notarios, document preparers, and fake lawyers. They say they can help, but they actually are not qualified to do so. Not only does the victim usually lose a lot of money, but they can also be in real trouble with the government. Most of these scams involve committing fraud by filing for certain immigration benefits they are not eligible for. Always seek out the opinion of an experienced immigration attorney to avoid being a victim of one of these scams.

Keep in mind that in most states, hiring a paralegal is a legal violation because paralegals must work under the direct supervision of an attorney. They cannot independently or directly provide legal services to the public. Any document preparer or business that is offering services directly to the public and says they are a paralegal is most likely in violation of state rules or is practicing the law illegally.

Using the term "notary" in a language other than English also normally indicates that state rules are being broken. (For example, in Spanish a notary public can be called a notario, escribano, or notario público.) In most States, a notary public cannot use their title to imply or create the idea that they are authorized to practice law.

Chapter 13:
Overcoming Fear

"Do the thing you fear to do and keep on doing it... that is the quickest and surest way ever yet discovered to conquer fear."

- **Dale Carnegie**

Do Not Let Fear Control You

If I could identify the biggest problem that affects people during the immigration process, it would be letting fear control them. Let me start by saying that having fear is normal. When you first become aware of something, being afraid of it is a typical, normal reaction. The bravest of people has fear. Fear of the unknown is very common. The problem starts when you let that fear control you. There are so many books about how to avoid letting fear control your actions. Find them and read them—not just for your immigration issue, but for all of life's issues. You will be a better person because of it.

As an attorney helping people with their immigration cases, I see fear in my clients all the time. They are afraid to do things because of a petrifying fear of the unknown. Imaginary scenarios make them lose sleep at night. I've known people who could have applied for certain benefits with the immigration authorities for several years. But because of fear, they never sought out help. They didn't even find out if they *could* take action.

After many years in the United States, people come into see me because they finally overcame their fear of just talking to a professional. I've had many clients who were in this situation. After I reviewed their case, I was happy to tell them that they had been eligible to apply for certain benefits for years, and they could do so immediately. So many clients have found themselves in problems that they could have avoided—if they had overcome their fear and gone to speak to a professional about helping them. One of the best pieces of advice that I can give you is to learn to overcome your fear.

My staff and I approach every client that walks into my office with the idea that first and foremost, we want to help them and educate them. So in all of my consultations, the first thing I do is get as much information as possible from the client. Once I have all the information I need, I can make a very clear, thorough analysis of the case. Then I can better advise them about how I can help them. I can show them what specific benefits they are eligible for that will help them or their family, what to do to get started with the application process, and how to avoid deportation.

Even if a client never hires me to help them, the one thing I can say is that while they are in my office, they will be educated and informed about their standing. Then they will know what they *can* do. They will always walk out of my office more informed than when they walked in.

How to Overcome Fear

The best way to begin overcoming your fear is by become aware of what is causing that fear. When you should be taking action, fear causes inaction. Fear petrifies a person to the point that they can even get sick from it. Because of fear, people allow themselves to live miserably, instead of choosing to be happy. So identifying the reason for the fear starts the process.

Next comes looking for solutions. You can focus on the problem or the solution. Find the solution, and start working on a way to accomplish it. This forward-thinking, positive action will begin to melt away the fear. Overcoming fear does not happen instantly or automatically. It comes from a conscious action and a deliberate intention toward doing things that scare you. As you slowly learn about overcoming your fears and begin working on them, you grow as a person and expand all of the possibilities in your life.

Believe in yourself. Don't let doubt fill your mind. It will steal your joy, as well as the possibilities of a bright future.

Take Action

"If you want to conquer fear, don't sit home and think about it. Go out and get busy."

- **Dale Carnegie**

Do something that scares you. Are you afraid because you *might* hear bad news if you go see an attorney about your case? Go see the attorney! Go find out exactly what you are facing as a result of your situation or status. Educate yourself. Learn. Don't stand still. Even if you think you are going to die from fear, take action. Move forward. Little by little, you can overcome fear.

The results can be fantastic. Not only do you feel empowered, you also grow as a person. You learn to apply that newfound boldness to other fears and to other areas of your life. Suddenly, you notice that you don't live in fear of everything so much. You start to see things differently. One day, you wake up and realize that you are actually happier.

I have seen the transformation in so many of my client's lives—after they take their first step in overcoming their fears about their immigration case or situation. I have seen their faces change. These men and women looked much older than they actually were, but their appearance transformed. Now they look years younger. In some cases, this happens almost right away. In others, it is gradual—as the client accepts the good news I've given them, and that knowledge is slowly absorbed into their minds. When they accept the truth and believe in the possibilities available to them, it changes them into a new person. Years of fear and doubt are gone. A new hope is born in them.

Most likely, you are reading this book because you or your loved one has an immigration case that is of concern to you. If you are living in fear because of an immigration case, start to make an intentional choice to overcome it now. Begin by learning. Study all you can about the case. Know the details. The worst thing is a fear of the unknown. Shed light on that fear by educating yourself. You can start by going to see an attorney. Go well-prepared with the facts about the case, and learn from that attorney. Inform yourself.

Then apply the knowledge. If there is a solution, start working as hard as you can on making that solution happen. When you look back, you may find yourself angry that you were ever so fearful. That monster that once looked so big is now just a tiny, little insect. In that moment of realization, you will know that you overcame your fear. There are no words that can truly describe that feeling. It is a quiet calmness that fills you. No one can take it away from you. From that moment on, you are a new person.

Chapter 14:
Do I Really Need a Lawyer?

"He who represents himself has a fool for a client."

- **19th Century Proverb**

Should I hire a lawyer?

I have been asked this question by so many different people. The truth is that there is no law that says that you must hire a lawyer. You can take on any legal process involving an immigration case on your own.

But do you really want to do that? Do you know what you're doing? Are you prepared to fill out all of the paperwork yourself? What if you get confused? What if you can't figure it out? What if the government misplaces part—or even all—of your application? What if they pester you for documents that don't exist, or that you don't believe you should have to provide? It happens all the time.

So the correct question to ask is the original one: Should I hire a lawyer? Now more than ever, my answer is a resounding yes! Sometimes my potential clients look at that answer with suspicion, because they think that I am just trying to talk them into hiring me. If they are going to hire a lawyer, of course I would like to be the one they hire. But what I keep telling them is that whether it is me or any other attorney, they should hire a legitimate lawyer to help them with their case. The important thing is that

77

they get good, sound legal representation with their case. Whether it is a basic case or a complex one, having an experienced immigration attorney can be the wisest thing they do.

Being people, we all naturally have human emotions. And when we're dealing with our own life issues (whether they involve the law, finances, or family), these emotions can easily cloud the thinking of even the most intelligent person. An attorney can see things clearly, without the haze of emotions. Attorneys understand how to properly file court documents and handle other legal procedures. These days, I advise you to get an attorney for everything involving immigration law. The reason why is because even simple applications have recently been known to blow up into complex cases. Immigration law is complex, even for cases that are normally seen as simple.

All professionals, including lawyers, doctors, accountants, and dentists, have one thing in common: They all have years of education and training. Depending on the state they practice in, lawyers must usually complete continuing education every year. This training and education helps us keep up with the changes in the law, and it is used objectively. The intention is to constantly improve our skills, so we can represent our clients to the fullest. This continuing learning process can—and often does—make the difference between winning and losing a case.

Representing yourself can lead to detrimental results. I had a case in which a woman was being petitioned by her son. That seemed like a pretty straightforward type of application. She hired me to prepare the application, and it was filed. We reviewed the entire case. I had an extensive interview with her during the preparation for filing.

However, she did not continue with my representation when she went to the interview with USCIS. Instead, she chose to represent herself before the interviewing officer. At the interview, she was questioned about a previous filing for legal residence status, which she'd made based on her marriage to a man who had since passed away. Her application was subsequently denied; in that previous application, certain discrepancies were discovered, which made it seem as though her marriage to that husband was entered into just so she could get her immigration papers.

The file the government had on her from all those years earlier showed that she and her now-deceased husband were interviewed twice. And all those years ago, it was determined that she had filed a fraudulent application. Even though she was never told of that determination, it affected her ability to be approved for the petition that her son filed for her.

When she came into my office to review the denial, I asked her why she hadn't told me everything about that case. She replied that she did not think it was important, and that she didn't remember it that way.

In another case of mine, a man applied for naturalization, after having been a legal permanent resident for a little over 5 years. Everything was going well in his application, until he arrived at the interview without an attorney. There, it was revealed that they had discovered that he entered the U.S. as the husband of a wife that had been given asylum. The problem was that he divorced that wife just before he entered the United. The naturalization application was denied because he legally could not have entered the U.S. as a derivative of his wife's application and so his legal permanent resident status was given to him in error.

As an attorney, I have personally dealt with examples of cases like these numerous times. The common denominator in most of these cases is that these problems could have been avoided with the proper preparation of paperwork or the presence of a lawyer.

Some people see the idea of hiring an attorney as an unnecessary expense. They associate the idea of having an attorney as something extravagant. The proper way to look at it is to see an attorney as someone who can provide you with peace of mind, proper guidance, and knowledge. Then you can make sure that whatever process who have hired them to do is done accurately and correctly, and mistakes and future problems will be avoided.

Maximizing the possibility of a successful outcome in your case should be seen as an investment. We are talking about your life and your future—or that of your family. This is not the time to be frugal. Not having an experienced lawyer to assist you in your case may wind up costing you much more in the long run.

You'll hire me as your attorney because I can help you. I can greatly improve the chances that your case will succeed. I can make sure that your file is given proper consideration by the authorities. And if it isn't, I will litigate or do what it takes to have it treated fairly. The government has their officers and their attorneys, and you should have yours.

Summary

Should you hire an attorney for your immigration matter? My answer to that question is invariably yes, you should. You need good legal representation. If you are in deportation proceedings, it would be foolish not to have an attorney. If you want peace of mind, accuracy, and a better chance of success, then get an attorney.

In my office, we do most processes several times a month. But our clients will possibly only encounter an immigration case once in their entire lives. Wouldn't it make sense to hire someone who knows how to properly help you through your process?

Hiring Me for Your Case

Have you found yourself in need of help with an immigration case? Are you facing a deportation case in front of an immigration court? Do you have an application that needs to be filed for yourself or a family member? Do you already have one that has been filed with the government?

For these situations or any other type of immigration matter, you can call my office for help from anywhere in the country. My office is prepared to deal with anyone from anywhere via all modern technology, including the internet, teleconferencing, video conferencing, and onsite interviews. Don't let fear stop you from seeking professional help. It may make all the difference.

When I consult with a client for the first time, my goal is to learn all I can about the details of their case. With this information, I can accurately counsel them about how I can help them. Here's my promise to my clients: After a consultation with me, you will be educated about your case, and you will have a clear understanding about what can be done.

Since being admitted to the bar as an attorney in 1991, I have handled thousands of cases, and I have always focused on representing my clients by using every legal tool available to achieve success. The primary, specific area of focus in my practice has been immigration law. Even after over two decades of vast, professional experience and exposure, I am still personally involved in each of my office's cases. If I decide to represent you, I will be involved in your case!

Call today and set up a free initial consultation.
It could be one of the wisest decision you'll ever make.

Abraham B. Cardenas, Immigration Attorney

Phone: 717-801-1661

Email: cardenas@cardenaslawfirm.com

Website: www.CardenasLawFirm.com

Offices in Miami, Florida
1414 NW 107 Avenue, Suite 203
Miami, Florida 33172

Offices in York, Pennsylvania
18 South George Street, Suite 615
York, Pennsylvania 17401